Backyard Blessings

Stories from the Life
of Martha Wilson Jones

With Marianne Craft and Hyland Justice

Illustrated by Susan Welsh

Published by Looking Glass Books

Decatur, Georgia

Copyright © 2003 Martha Wilson Jones

All rights reserved. No part of this book may be reproduced in any form or by any means without prior written permission from the publisher, except in connection with reviews written specifically for inclusion in a magazine or newspaper.

Scripture quotations are from
Holy Bible: New International Version
Copyright © 1973, 1978, 1984 by International Bible Society

ISBN 1-929619-16-2

This book is dedicated to the Glory of God.

Backyard Blessings

ACKNOWLEDGMENTS

I would first like to give thanks and praise to our Heavenly Father, who breathed life into this project and saw it to completion. He has so graciously answered prayer after prayer and his Spirit has connected and sustained us.

Marianne Craft and Hyland Justice suggested the idea of a book of reflections from my life. They headed up the huge task of organizing our taping sessions, writing, editing, and coordinating the myriad details that have gone into making this a reality.

Ruth Ann Skinner typed and edited along the way. Most importantly, she took the almost finished text and with a keen and fresh eye edited and polished the manuscript to its finished form.

Nancy McGuirk beautifully matched the scriptures to the text. In addition, she read and reread many drafts giving sound advice and much encouragement.

Ree Hoffman typed, edited, proofread, and ran errands on a moment's notice. Her joyful spirit uplifted and encouraged all of us during our journey together.

I would like to thank our artist and friend Susan Welsh. She so graciously and generously shared her gift of creativity designing the beautiful and perfect cover as well as the exquisite inside drawings. Her work reflects not only her time and talent, but her passion for art, life, and friends. And last but not least, many thanks go to our publisher and friend, Dick Parker. He guided and shaped this endeavor with infinite patience and great kindness.

I love you all and am deeply grateful for your gifts of time and love.

Martha Wilson Jones

INTRODUCTION

For decades, Martha Wilson Jones' wit, wise counsel, and deep faith, have touched many people of all ages. In the spring of 2000, two of her friends, who had been deeply inspired by her faith and wisdom, felt called to chronicle God's abiding presence in her life throughout nearly one hundred years of joyous and difficult times. Thus, a three year adventure began with three additional close friends of Martha's joining the original two.

The six of us gathered in Martha's sunny, plant filled apartment, which still smelled of fresh paint. She had recently moved there, after living fifty-eight years in her beloved family home where she had led a bustling life as a wife, mother, piano teacher, and avid gardener. We marveled at the warmth and order her new home conveyed and felt as if she had lived there for years.

As we nestled into comfortable chairs to begin our time together, we were filled with a sense of deep respect and unending admiration for our amazing friend, Martha. The twinkle in her eye combined with her beautiful smile and warm, accepting manner gave us a sense of peace and anticipation.

Martha, ninety-seven years old, was the wisest person any of us knew. She had been teaching the Bible for over sixty years, was in perfect health, had an agile and sharp mind, and had experienced most of life's many challenges. Her sense of humor permeated her reflections, and her depth of character was revealed in her continued spiritual growth through trials and triumphs.

We longed to know and understand this growth. What was her secret? How might she be able to advise us as we traveled on our own personal journeys? We knew she had experienced the difficulties and heartaches of a long life, yet her unfailing faith had always sustained her from the valleys to the mountaintops. She was indeed our treasure-chest friend.

Martha had been married to Gene Wilson, pastor of Peachtree Presbyterian Church (now the largest Presbyterian church in the country) for forty-eight years. He and Martha had arrived in Atlanta in 1936 and Gene had shepherded the then very small church out of bankruptcy.

Gene had died of lung cancer, and at age seventy-eight Martha had married a longtime friend, Fred Jones, who was then eighty-four. We knew her daughter Peggy had suffered a debilitating stroke at the age of fifty-three, and we knew Martha's son Gene had polio as a teenager. Witnessing the great suffering of two children had left Martha heartbroken.

We longed to know what had sustained her and kept her intact through the turmoil of heartache and the rigors of disappointment. What had kept her smiling, and why was she not left with the bitterness and resentment that we had seen in others?

What could possibly have imprinted this positive outlook? Our questions that day began a wondrous journey with Martha through her fascinating and unpredictable life. We met every other week for nine months asking questions, listening to stories, and seeking answers for the struggles that we all invariably bump up against in our own lives.

By the time we finished, we had relived with Martha most of her years here on earth. Our hope was that we could emulate her and move through our own lives with the same unfailing spirit and grace.

Her beautiful spirit and humble grace were to us the unspoken sermon of a life built on the foundation of an unwavering faith in her Lord and Savior, Jesus Christ. Her irresistible charm was a reflection of the ageless song we all learn as children, "Jesus Loves Me."

This book is a collection of some of the memories shared by our treasured friend. It is written with much love and Martha's hope that it will glorify God and inspire all who read it to examine their own faith journey.

Backyard Blessings

*Then will all your people be righteous and they will possess
the land forever. They are the shoot I have planted, the
work of my hands, for the display of my splendor.*
Isaiah 60:21

BACKYARD BLESSINGS

*"Listen! A farmer went out to sow his seed. As he was
scattering the seed, some fell along the path, and the birds
came and ate it up. Some fell on rocky places, where it did
not have much soil. It sprang up quickly, because the soil
was shallow. But when the sun came up, the plants were
scorched, and they withered because they had no root.
Other seed fell among thorns, which grew up and choked
the plants, so that they did not bear grain. Still other seed
fell on good soil. It came up, grew and produced a crop,
multiplying thirty, sixty, or even a hundred times."*
Then Jesus said, "He who has ears to hear, let him hear."
MARK 4:3-9

One of God's dearest gifts to me has been my garden. Each day a miracle of nature occurs in God's inani-
mate world. It makes no difference if it is a small or
large flower garden, a small or large vegetable garden, a
city garden, or a country garden. A dry, dead seed is

planted in the ground, nourished with sun and rain, and is resurrected into new life in a short period of time. Seeing this miracle occur time and time again through flowers, plants, and vegetables touched me spiritually and emotionally in a way that is hard to describe. Gardening allowed me to retreat to a place that not only satisfied my need for color and beauty but also made me draw closer to God.

Our three children were quite close in age, and whether they were toddlers or teenagers, there were always many demands. During the thirteen years my mother lived with us, I also taught Sunday school and piano, and was a wife, a mother, and a friend to many.

Most of the time life was a joy, but every so often I would just want to tear my hair out! Instead, I would go out to my backyard and work in the garden. I would do the hard digging and weeding and would return to my house physically exhausted. Really I was burying many ugly thoughts and grumpy dispositions in all those holes! So you see, not only did the garden satisfy me spiritu-

ally and physically, it was also a wonderful place to release all of my pent-up emotions.

In the beauty of the quiet mornings I could have
time alone, which for many years was hard to find. I
didn't need a book or my Bible to have a devotional
because being in a place that was quiet and lovely met a
need in me that nothing else could satisfy. I thanked
God for it every day.

Something else particularly lovely about my garden
was that in a few short years after planting, I always had
something to share with others. There were enough flowers to take to sick friends, to enjoy in my home, or flowers to give to friends when they came to visit. When I
was ready to prune, separate, clean out, and divide, there
was usually someone who wanted a little something.
There is still a bit of my garden all around the Buckhead
area.

So many of my flowers were given to me, and nur-
turing them and then passing them on to friends gave
me such a nice feeling. It was a tangible way to share

my love with others. But undoubtedly, the biggest blessing I received was gradually being able to understand God's complete love for his children through this amazing process of planting and nourishing a garden.

Let me explain. A garden is a perfect mix of many different flowers—roses, dahlias, lilies, and many others. Some are large and colorful and make quite a splash in the overall setting. Others are smaller and less colorful, but without them the garden would be incomplete. I had a ground cover that consisted of the most delicate daisies you have ever seen. They had the tiniest petals with a little pin dot of yellow in the middle, were absolutely perfect, and covered the ground in such a lovely way. Without them the bare soil would have been quite unattractive.

Gardening taught me that one does not have to be important and accomplished, as defined by our world. If you are true to the way God made you, then you are as perfect as you can be. Some of us can't be the big dahlia or the striking rose. These flowers are indeed beautiful, but the garden would be quite unfinished without the little daisy ground cover. By seeing the significant value of each individual plant, I've been able to see the value of each person. It doesn't matter whether a person is in the forefront or quietly working in the background, they are all of equal importance.

Sometimes it takes an adjustment to realize that truth and to recognize that it is all right to be in the background. Ordinary gifts are just as valuable as the more recognized ones. That is indeed the way God planned it, everyone having his or her own unique gifts and talents, each one necessary to complete God's plan, each one necessary to make the body of Christ whole, each one valued and needed to perfect the garden. Not only did I learn to accept myself and others through these simple garden lessons, I learned to accept and adjust to the disappointments and heartaches that came along the way.

Soil does not bring forth abundantly unless it is turned upside down and inside out. It must be completely loosened in order for the roots to grow down deep. This necessary upheaval is also true in our lives. We often don't let God's spirit or God's love into our lives until we hit bottom, until we've been turned upside down and inside out as the soil of the earth is turned.

Flowers must be constantly weeded and pruned to bear fruit. We are the same way. We must live through our tragedies, temptations, and sorrows in order to fully appreciate our blessings and to give praise to our Heavenly Father, who is the giver of all good gifts. Pruning must be done in order to keep the shape and quality of plants at their best. We as God's children also need pruning in order to be our best.

Like the soil, we must go through upheaval to allow our roots to grow deep in the unshakable soil of God's love, mercy, and grace. The dogwood's tiny bud must endure the winter's cold before it can open to the sun's warmth at springtime. Often, we too must experience the cold and bitter times before our hearts can be opened to the warmth and love Christ has waiting for us.

Various flowers require different seasons, climates, and soils for propagation. Some do beautifully in sand; others need loam; some need full sun, others only shade. Some need dry, arid conditions, while others require much rain. Then there are those that need a great deal of room to grow, while others flourish best in crowded conditions.

And so it is with us. We all bloom at different seasons, in different places, and with different gifts. Because of God's great wisdom and design, his plan can be continuously carried out in many places using many people. How good he is to have taught me so many of life's lessons right in my own backyard. It was indeed a backyard of blessings.

The Blessing of Love

Love is patient, love is kind. It does not envy, it does not boast, it is not proud. It is not rude, it is not self-seeking, it is not easily angered, it keeps no record of wrongs. Love does not delight in evil but rejoices with the truth. It always protects, always trusts, always hopes, always perseveres. Love never fails.

1 Corinthians 13:4-8

Sowing Seeds of Love

*These commandments I give to you today are to be upon
your hearts. Impress them on your children. Talk about
them when you sit at home and when you walk along the
road, when you lie down and when you get up.*

Deuteronomy 6:6, 7

I can hardly believe that I was born nearly a century
ago—in 1906, actually. I spent my early years in Aiken,
South Carolina, where my father was the pastor of the
Presbyterian church. Remarkably, so many memories
from back then are as fresh as if they were yesterday, yet
the love shared within my family remains the most precious of all. Isn't it funny that financial hardship, life-
threatening illness, strict discipline, and hard work not
only shaped my character, but also increased the love
and respect for one another within my family? However, I wouldn't be honest if I did not admit that it is a
lot easier to look back from my present-day perspective

than it was to live through some of those difficult times.

I clearly recall our little manse which sat upon church property located at the intersection of two dusty main roads in Aiken. It was certainly small by today's standards, yet we had a screened porch that wrapped around the front and right side of the house, which was a comfortable expansion of our living space. My three brothers and I played and slept out there, and we eavesdropped on those who visited as they rocked back and forth in creaky old wooden rockers.

In fact, it was while on the porch one day that we first heard an automobile approaching our intersection. How could it be that something so commonplace in today's world created such excitement, fear, and trembling in three small children nearly a century ago? But it surely did. That Model T rumbling and bumping up the dusty, rain-riveted road was like an apparition beyond our most vivid imaginings. After all, walking, cycling, and buggy rides or horseback riding were the only modes of transportation back then. For most families an automobile was a frivolous luxury .

First Corinthians 13 clearly states that without love we have nothing. In our family, considering all of the material possessions at our fingertips today, we had almost nothing—yet we did have an abundance of love. I recall many illustrations of the committed love we had for one another, the most vivid being when I was stricken with dreaded typhoid fever, so often fatal in the early 1900s. My parents labored for days tucking icepacks around me to bring down my deliriously high fever, and encouraging me to suck on ice chips to avoid dehydration, which was then life threatening to small children. They applied poultices, patiently fed me herbal potions teaspoonful by teaspoonful—and prayed. Antibiotics were unheard of, and survival more frequently than not, depended on the loving care of those around us. I have no doubt that my parent's attention, love, prayers, and discipline saved my life.

I was a feisty child, and, as I regained my strength, I was devastated to learn that my head would have to be shaved since the high fever had caused my hair to fall out in large clumps. Oh, how I wept and wailed as the town barber shaved my head with a straight razor. Surely I would be the only seven year old in town with a bald head! Before long a lovely little hat was purchased for me to wear to school and church, and eventually, as Mother had confidently promised in spite of my doubts, my hair grew back uniformly thick and curly.

As young children are prone to be, my brothers and I were a pretty inquisitive, rambunctious crew left primarily to our mother to corral and tame. Our father's schedule was demanding and often grueling. While he and mother were of one accord in their philosophy of child rearing, he was, of necessity, frequently absent. While Daddy was busy presiding over weddings and funerals, planning his Sunday sermons, and responding to the many and varied needs of our community, Mother was equally busy rounding up us children, and parceling out chores and activities to keep us out of trouble. In small communities in those days, a minister and his family were kept under watchful scrutiny, so it was no small feat for her to keep us toeing the line single-handedly. But toe the line we did, and I can assure you we did it respectfully and obediently because we certainly knew the consequences if we didn't!

A day in the life of Pastor Johnston's family in 1915 went something like this: Mother would rouse us early in the morning and, after washing and dressing, we all congregated in the kitchen for morning prayers and a hearty breakfast. Morning prayers were a must for our family, not because Daddy was a pastor but because our parents were genuinely devoted to God and the teachings of his Son, Jesus Christ. It was vital to both of them that their deep faith be imparted to each of us, so we were raised according to loving Christian principles. Following breakfast, depending on whether school was in session, we began our morning chores. As soon as they were completed, since we didn't own a radio, a Victrola (which was a hand cranked record player), or have access to a newspaper, Mother created activities for us that kept us productively engaged for hours on end. She was a gifted teacher, and we never lacked for spiritual, intellectual, or cultural stimulation.

Mother never wavered in her belief that material abundance was unnecessary and that knowing Jesus Christ, his teachings, and his love for us, was of foremost importance. For example, a lesson for the day might have been on tithing. Being a natural teacher, she was never short of examples for our daily lessons . . . like when I earned ten pennies to buy two glorious ice cream cones, she managed to convince me (oh so sweetly) to put one penny in our family tithing box. It was a lesson I never forgot because of the manner in which she suggested it.

My siblings and I felt quite secure in the definitive structure of our family and the obvious devotion our parents had for one another and for us. They were determined, also, that each one of us have an excellent education. To achieve this, every single unnecessary item was eliminated from their budget so that each penny saved was deposited into our education funds.

Reflecting on my life as I was growing up, I'm grateful that my parents were committed to actively model 1 Corinthians 13. Their lives were a witness to this scripture, not only within our family, but in the way they touched so many other people over the years. A solid foundation of love was laid that carried all of us children through myriad adversities and joyous celebrations. This was a lasting legacy and one that we have all tried to pass down to our own children.

THE MIRACLE OF CHILDREN

Sons are a heritage from the Lord…like arrows in the
hand of a warrior…blessed is the man whose
quiver is full of them.
PSALM 127:3-5

The birth of a child seems almost commonplace, an incidental everyday occurrence that typically results in great happiness for those who are most closely related. The arrival of a newborn baby usually calls for a round of celebratory events and a flurry of gift giving. Then the excitement diminishes as we find ourselves, more or less, returning to old routines. Somehow, the grand miracle of new life seems to fade unless we take the time to reflect on this truly precious and remarkable gift from God. The births of each of my children—Beth, Peggy, and Gene—were the three greatest milestones of my life.

Our firstborn, Beth, represented my first real sense of working a miracle with God. It was just all so new to me! She was truly a squirming piece of perfection, from her tiny, manicured fingernails and toenails to her perfect nose and pink rosebud of a mouth. As I lay in my hospital bed following her birth, I simply could not believe that this little seven-and-a-half pound person began with a cell too small to visualize with the human eye.

I hadn't been able to conceptualize what it would be like to see and hold our beautifully formed child who had lived in my womb for nine months. I became exquisitely aware that she had everything she needed in order to live her life as God created her. She had been born with a preordained body, intelligence, and the senses she would need to achieve whatever she desired in her life on this earth.

Of course, I didn't know at the time if all of this would come to fruition but I did have a real sense of the possibilities, and an awareness of being closer to God than I had ever been. I reflected on passages from Isaiah and Daniel, "Before they call I will answer; while they are speaking, I will hear" (Isaiah 65:24). God had used his miraculous power in bringing Beth to life; she had come from a tiny seed, and had grown into a form that lived in the womb for nine months. Then through the equally miraculous process of birth, she came to life and was placed in my arms to cherish and to raise.

I had prayed, with great fervor, for the health and well-being of all of my children—and I then had prayed for some specifics. One of my most heartfelt prayers was that they would be blessed with some measure of musical ability, since music was a vital part of my own life. I was touched, and in awe, when God faithfully answered my prayers, beginning with Beth. It was then I began to recognize how deeply personal my relationship with him was becoming because I could see what a great work he was doing in so many facets of my life.

The first evidence of Beth's interest in music is indelible in my memory, even though it occurred nearly seven decades ago. It was a wondrous thing, when as a small toddler, her tiny fingers found the white keys of our piano. Even had I wanted to, I couldn't have kept her away from the piano. Soon she began to create little tuneful melodies. In answer to my prayers, all three of our children have been blessed with amazing gifts of musical ability.

I continue to be in awe of the remarkable miracle of our children. When holding a new baby, we can see a bright glimpse of God's unconditional love for His own people. But it is in the growth and development of all our children that we can sense his abiding presence and plan for all of his creation.

GROWING A CHURCH

I am the vine; you are the branches. If a man remains in
me and I in him, he will bear much fruit; apart from me
you can do nothing. If you remain in me and my words
remain in you, ask whatever you wish, and it will be given
you. This is to my father's glory, that you bear much fruit,
showing yourselves to be my disciples.
JOHN 15:5,7-8

Often God has such a quiet manner of directing and
protecting us that it is only with hindsight we're able to
see his hand in certain situations.

Gene never doubted his call to the ministry, and I
never doubted that God called me to be Gene's wife. It
was with this confidence and faith that we set off from
Walhalla, South Carolina, with our two small daughters
bound for our new pastorate in Atlanta. The year was

1936 and we found ourselves traveling into one of the worst ice storms ever to hit the southeastern states. We were in an old car with no heat, sliding along rural back roads, never doubting that we were doing what we were supposed to be doing. Our children were snugly wrapped, with hot water bottles tucked around them, which kept them relatively warm until we reached Jefferson, Georgia. Gene deposited us with my parents and picked up my brother, Frank, and they continued on to Atlanta.

In those days, traveling by car was always a difficult challenge, but on icy roads without heat it was a true exercise in faith! Gene and Frank never wavered, even as they skidded into gulches and slid along the roads as if on ice skates. Eventually they arrived in Atlanta to find downed power lines, no phones, and a locked up, very dark manse in the heart of Buckhead. Thus was Gene's dramatic entrance into a new city, to serve a new church, and to begin a new life for himself and his young family.

Today I have no doubt that God was in that car every treacherous mile of the way, for he had much larger plans for us and our young church than we could ever have anticipated.

Peachtree Presbyterian Church, in 1936, was a rather small building constructed of rough-hewn stone mined from Stone Mountain granite. Upon arriving, Gene was dismayed to find that not only was there no roster of members, but the church was in dire structural and financial condition. In looking back, God knew exactly who he was selecting to grow a small, financially unstable church. Gene loved nothing better than a seemingly impossible challenge. The Great Depression in the 1930s had depleted people's resources and financially ruined many institutions. Thus our little church wound up being sold to some New Orleans bankers on the courthouse steps. And so, the challenge was on!

Gene dearly loved people and his initial decision, amidst all the turmoil, was to engage a small group of men with financial backgrounds to assist him in negotiating with the New Orleans bankers to buy back our church. His next task was to contact all church members to pray for God's direction which, without a roster, was no small feat.

Little by little, he began building a roll of active members and, in talking with them, acquired the names of other members who had wandered away. These were active young members who, unable to provide much financial assistance, nevertheless banded together with a burning desire to save the church.

God was present in this endeavor beyond our wildest dreams. As our church membership began to grow, tithing took on an entirely new meaning. The mostly young, financially strapped families made a committed decision to do without many basic necessities in order to buy back our church from the New Orleans bankers. Additionally, three major Atlanta churches each offered to aid us with $10,000. That's when Gene, with the support of his financial committee, went to New Orleans in an attempt to work things out with the bank, promising to pay $30,000 in cash up front and the remainder over a manageable period of time. The balance would be paid through membership pledges.

I must say that for quite a long time not many of us showed up at church clothed in the latest styles! We pulled together in such an extraordinary way that in just a few years we were no longer in debt. From that point, God began to grow our congregation far more rapidly than we had ever anticipated, and, fourteen years later, in 1960, we moved, debt free, to a brand new building around the corner from the original church.

It is written in Isaiah 28:16 that God has laid "a precious cornerstone for a sure foundation." For our struggling little church, Jesus Christ was indeed that cornerstone.

God's faithful presence, and the abiding faith of our congregation through uncertainty, adversity, and financial difficulties, were beautiful witnesses to his ultimate design for our church community.

GOD'S UNCONDITIONAL LOVE
AT ITS BEST

*"Above all, love each other deeply because love covers
a multitude of sins."*
I PETER 4:8

In the 1940s life was hectic and unpredictable in many respects, and that certainly extended over to our household of two busy parents and three active children. The church was growing rapidly, and the demands on Gene were constant and challenging. I was trying to be his helpmate while attempting to effectively mother our small children and teach piano to supplement our income. Frustratingly, household chores and cooking just didn't seem to fit into the equation. That was when God brought the miracle of Sarah into our lives.

Sarah was a delightful, energetic woman in her thirties. She was married with no children, and she too wanted to supplement her income. Within no time she whipped our frazzled household into shape and solidly endeared herself to each member of our family. The children loved her so much that they begged Gene and me to go out in the evenings just so Sarah could spend an extended day with them.

In addition to restoring our lives to some measure of normalcy, her Southern cooking kept us far too fat and happy to ever take her for granted. Life just couldn't have been better.

For the nearly eight years she was a part of our family, Sarah was present most mornings to prepare breakfast for us. This enabled her to participate in our family's tradition of shared morning prayers and Gene's Bible readings. Little did we know that she had been absorbing all the scripture and prayers and had come to a faith of her own during our breakfast times together.

After Sarah left, we continued to stay in close touch. We learned many years later that her husband had an affair with another woman, and a child was born of that union. Sarah was devastated. However, she was called to do the unbelievable by forgiving her husband and taking his child into her home to raise as her own.

Sarah's experience is the greatest illustration of love I have seen in my lifetime. It's the kind of godly love that loves without expectation. It is love without pride or self-gratification and is, for that reason, superior to the love of a parent for his or her own child. Our own children reflect our training—a personal investment. They are inheritors of familial traits, and parental expectations are an inevitable part of the package. But God loves us even when we're unlovable. He loves us when we are entirely undeserving. That is how Sarah loved both her husband and his child. What Sarah did was impossible to do through her own human strength, yet in surrendering her great sorrow to the Lord, she was able to heal and forgive—a lesson to me which has been a lasting inspiration.

Although this is a story without an ending, there is a caveat. Many years later, when Sarah's health began to decline, it was her husband's child who lovingly and compassionately cared for her.

The Blessing of Forgiveness

And when you stand praying, if you hold anything against anyone, forgive him, so that your Father in heaven may forgive you your sins.

Mark 11:25

SOFTENING THE SOIL:
LESSONS ON FORGIVENESS

"Be kind and compassionate to one another, forgiving each other, just as in Christ God forgave you."
EPHESIANS 4:32

Learning about forgiveness and learning how to forgive have been difficult lessons for me. God has had to teach me gently and illustrate for me through some troubled times how important this forgiveness business really is.

I was born the first of five children into a fine Christian home. My parents had two great objectives for all of us. One was for us to know Jesus Christ as our personal Savior; the other was for all of us to receive a good education before leaving home. Everything else was sacrificed toward those two ideals and, as I matured, I realized what a great foundation had been laid for me.

I decided on my own that I would never marry a preacher, that I would never teach Sunday school, and that my life's work was to be a minister of music in some nice church. But God had different ideas completely!

He sent Gene Wilson my way, which turned out to be the end of not being a preacher's wife. I decided that life would not be worth living if it couldn't be with Gene. Then God closed all the doors when I tried to prepare to be a leader of music in a church. My life was beginning to be turned around in so many ways that I was no longer clear as to what my gifts really were and how I was to serve.

God gave me one gift, though, that was very clear. It was the gift of unending gab. I could talk a blue streak about anything to the point of boredom! A gift can be both a blessing and a curse, and I had particular struggles with this gift.

I left college with a poignant reminder of how my loose tongue could get me into trouble. During my senior year at Agnes Scott, I said some ugly and unkind things about someone I really loved and admired. In all tears and sincerity I went to her and asked her to forgive me. She emphatically stated that forgiveness was not part of her nature. I had lost a friend and was absolutely miserable.

One would think that I had learned my lesson, but I had not. After Gene and I were married and in our first pastorate, I talked myself into a corner and had to tell a small lie to get out of it. At first I considered it just happenstance, but God soon nudged my conscience. Every morning I would wake up and think, "Martha, you are a liar." Guilt and disappointment in myself nearly tore me apart, so finally I quietly met God and asked him to forgive me. This is not something that I'm proud of, but it is important, because it was my first real experience with God person to person.

You see, I had left home with my mother's and father's faith. I had been tempted in small ways all through high school and college. But to be a minister's wife, to have been called to service through my love for Gene, and then to have failed in that respect was a humbling experience.

But through this experience I learned that all those beautiful verses in the Bible about confessing your sins are true. God is just and righteous, I learned, and will forgive your sins and cleanse you. I began to understand the petition in the Lord's Prayer written in Matthew 6:9 to "lead us not into temptation but deliver us from evil." Understanding these passages made such a difference in my life, and God became very real to me for the first time.

In the early years as a minister's wife, I was on the receiving end of some bitter words. Someone said something cruel, untrue, vulgar, and dirty. My anger just came surging up; I wanted to swing out and slap this person in the face. But young minister's wives don't go around slapping other people in the face, especially at Presbyterian women's meetings! So I had to deal with my anger and feelings of hatred and all the mean, ugly things Christians aren't supposed to have in their hearts.

A year or two later this same woman called me to come by and see her. I readily accepted the invitation. Imagine my shock at learning the devastating news that she had only a few more months to live.

As I sat by her bed and held her hand, we began to sing hymns together—favorite ones like "The Old Rugged Cross" and other hymns of praise and worship. In that time together, God cleansed my heart. You know, you can't sing hymns with a woman who is going to die without forgiving her!

And so I thanked God. I had certainly experienced all aspects of this loose tongue business. I had not been forgiven by a friend, but I had been forgiven by God. In turn, I had forgiven someone else. Maybe I was beginning to understand what it meant to live as a Christian.

Forgiving means giving up the desire for revenge and letting go of the anger and resentment, trusting that God will make things right. The release and the cleansing that follows is exhilarating. Although God requires of us much that is difficult, he shows us the way we can follow him in obedience.

Only Christ who lives in us is able to do this impossible task of forgiveness. We only have to yield our stubborn nature to him and let him work within us. It is in this yielding that we are able to forgive others and to experience God's mighty cleansing. One day we will have to stand before God and make an accounting. He is going to say, "How have you done in the forgiveness department?" It is written in Matthew 7:2, "For in the same way you judge others, you will be judged, and with the measure you use, it will be measured to you." This forgiveness business is a serious and tricky thing!

The Blessing of Friendship

Two are better than one, because they have a good return for their work: If one falls down, his friend can help him up. But pity the man who falls and has no one to help him up!

Ecclesiastes 4:9-10

FRIENDS OF ALL AGES
FOR ALL AGES

*A man of many companions may come to ruin, but there is
a friend who sticks closer than a brother.*
PROVERBS 18:24

In 1923, when I was a rising senior in high school,
my father was called to the Presbyterian Church in
Greensboro, Georgia. I was furious over being uprooted
at such an important time in my life. Being transplanted
to a small school with only twelve seniors was a trauma
almost beyond endurance and I became quite grave and
somber in my demeanor.

When one is the new person on the scene, especially in a small school, it isn't too difficult to rapidly
become acquainted with your peers, whether you want
to or not. I was certainly no exception to the general
rule of being excruciatingly scrutinized by a new class,

and I was miserable. Finding someone I liked with whom I might share my love of music seemed unimaginable. Life was pretty dismal.

After a week or two of being pitiful, I began to notice that one of the students in my class lived in our neighborhood. Elise was a rather pretty girl who seemed to have both presence and poise in and out of the classroom. Watching her, my curiosity was piqued, and I noticed that she was also watching me. Before long, we became fast friends and I was delighted to learn that she was a remarkably talented pianist.

At a point of youthful despair, God brought exactly the right person into my life, and Elise and I have remained friends throughout the past eighty years.

One of the important aspects of this experience was that I began to understand how God can reveal himself to us through our friends. Friendships have nourished my soul, strengthened me, and allowed me to see a bit of Jesus each day. My friends have sustained me, divided my sorrows, and multiplied my joys.

I like to remember the scripture, Luke 24:18, about the disciples on the road to Emmaus.

Jesus was with them, but they didn't realize it because they could not recognize him. This applies to us in everyday life. When we wonder where God is, when we don't see evidence of his existence and activity, we have to look for him in the things that are familiar to us. We may see him in other persons who cross our paths, in scripture, or in nature. Often in looking back, we are then able to recognize that he has been right beside us all along.

I am always so touched by God when I look at each of my friends. That is when I truly can see the fruits of the spirit and the gifts of the spirit given to each of us as described by Paul in Galations 5:12. I see the spirit of gentleness in some friends, the spirit of joy, or perhaps of meekness, and in others, the gift of healing. When I see people being compassionate, when they are teaching, serving, or preaching, there is clear evidence that God is at work furthering his Kingdom and completing the body of Christ here on earth.

Not long ago, an old friend of mine mentioned how lonely she was, which I genuinely understood. However, as we talked, I realized how fortunate I have been to have made a host of younger friends who mean the world to me. When I mentioned this to her, she wanted to know how I had made friends with so many younger people at our age in life! I explained that I had been teaching Sunday school almost all of my adult life, and that I'd set a goal of making at least one new friend every three months of teaching. As I continue to teach, I continue to make new friends and this practice has been my salvation.

At my age, most of my friends have died. They were friends with whom I had grown and matured spiritually and emotionally, the ones who had shared my greatest joys and sorrows along the way. Each time one of these precious friends died, I felt as if I was losing a part of myself—that I was no longer whole. To say that my more recent, younger friends have been my salvation is, indeed, an understatement. The encouragement and love from these new relationships in my life have enabled me to keep teaching and have given me a fresh anticipation for each new day. Each morning I wake up and say: "This is the day that I'm depending on you, God. Guide me, direct me, show me, and help me to recognize the opportunities." He has answered my prayer in countless ways—especially in giving me the privilege of playing an integral part in some of the unique journeys of my younger friends. I consider them to be one of God's greatest blessings.

CONFIDENTIALITY: A TREASURED COMMODITY

When words are many, sin is not absent, but he who holds his tongue is wise.
PROVERBS 10:19

Gene and I decided in the beginning of his ministry that it would be better for me not to have just one best friend within the church but to have many good friends. That way I had lots of people to be happy with, not just one. Because of that decision, I learned to enjoy all different kinds of people. I learned to find something I liked in all these various personalities so that I could get along with them. It is impossible to like everyone all the time, but I learned to love people in the Christian sense.

So often in close relationships we are tempted to share things that are not necessary or appropriate. Not having one best friend helped me in that area, but Gene also helped me in a tremendous way. Let me explain.

Gene's compassion toward others and his role as pastor made him the perfect person to seek for advice. He never spoke to me about any problems or confidences that people shared with him. "It's better for you not to know," he told me. "You could slip up and treat someone differently, so it's just better this way."

I soon learned what wisdom there was in that because early in Gene's ministry, a friend stopped me in the hall at church one day. She was convinced that I was aware of the difficulties she had shared with Gene in a counseling session. When I was unable to respond to some leading remarks she made, she actually accused me of lying. I laughed it off and went straight home to thank him for his high regard of confidentiality.

A Bigger Plan:
66 Years of Teaching

*"For I know the plans I have for you," declares the Lord,
"plans to prosper you and not to harm you, plans to give
you hope and a future."*
Jeremiah 29:11

In the 1940s during World War II, it was common
for nearly everyone to have vegetable gardens, backyard
chickens, or occasionally a pig or two. The government
had placed restrictions on many food staples, so people
in our country adapted by growing and raising much of
their own food.

Our church manse was on an acre plot of land, so
Gene and I felt blessed to be able to raise a fair amount
of food in our own backyard right in the suburbs of
Atlanta.

During the fall of 1942, when Gene attended a week
long seminar in New York City, I was left alone to take

care of our children, the garden and the pigs. I have a particular memory of an incident involving our pigs that still tickles me when I think about it. It happened on a Sunday morning when I was hustling about the house getting myself and the children dressed for church, trying to pull together all of my materials for teaching Sunday school.

We were just about ready to leave when I heard our two pigs loudly squealing in their pen. I rushed into the kitchen, threw together their feed (known as slop), and ran down the back stairs to their pen. As I shoved the large, heavy bucket over the top of the fence, one of the pigs jumped up in his usual haste to be the first to eat, pushing the bucket of slop all over me. I was covered from head to toe! I had to tear back inside the house to change all of my clothes and was furious with that pig.

I finally showed up to teach my Sunday school class; they had been singing the same songs over and over as they waited for me. Embarrassed and out of breath, I apologized for being late and explained my disastrous slopping of the pigs story, thinking it was pretty funny. Not one person in my class cracked a smile, and to this day, I think they were simply sung out.

The world, during those years, was in great turmoil because of the depression and war. It was a relief to find something to laugh about, and I enjoyed sharing humorous situations and funny stories with my friends. However, my deepest desire was to share my faith, which I tried to do in a gentle, yet specific way. However, it had never been my own personal plan to share my faith through teaching, especially in a classroom setting.

My experience teaching Sunday school began in an unexpected way about five years earlier, in the summer of 1937. A young couple expressed an interest in starting a couples' class and asked if I would temporarily teach it for six months while the teacher they had selected was out of town. I agreed to help out, thinking I could do just about anything for only six months. Little did I know that God had a much bigger plan, for had I known it was the beginning of a sixty-six year commit-ment, I would have told them "Absolutely not!"

At the time I had three small children, which made preparing a lesson and being available every Sunday a challenge. However, God provided for my needs in many unexpected ways, especially through our housekeeper, Sarah. With her help, I felt sure I could keep my prom-ise to teach for six months.

Our first class began on a lovely fall morning in October with two couples. Our church was small, and no classroom was available, so Gene generously offered his small study for us to use. The following week two more couples appeared, and so it went each week until we had outgrown his study and moved to the old stone manse behind the church. It wasn't long before we had 150 people attending regularly and we eventually wound up meeting in the church sanctuary.

Teaching felt very natural to me, and I particularly enjoyed the friendships that developed in our class. I felt accountable to all of the faithful people, who ranged from young parents to older retirees. I also felt as if my own life was changing dramatically.

Studying the material I was teaching was quite different from just reading or memorizing it, and I was committed to organizing everything in my mind. I knew if I didn't learn it well, I would be unable to teach it well, and I realized that I couldn't do all of it on my own without God's help. I prayerfully asked him for guidance and discipline each time I sat down to study, for I wanted only to be given the exact words from the Holy Spirit.

It didn't take long for me to realize I couldn't teach scripture without living what I was teaching, which meant making some changes in my own life. The message of the Bible became very personal to me. No longer was God's word something I had learned about in my home as a child, or in another book I had studied at Agnes Scott. The scriptures were now guiding me to live my life as God would have me live it.

In the sixty-six years that I have been teaching,

the importance of the Bible has grown with each lesson I have taught. It continues to humble me to recall my early years of growing up when I vowed that I would never be a teacher. I now realize that God has his own plan, one that he reveals to us in his time—not in our time.

God's Gift to Me

So do not fear, for I am with you; do not be dismayed, for I am your God. I will strengthen you and help you; I will uphold you with my righteous right hand.
Isaiah 41:10

I decided to take a break from teaching after Gene's death in May of 1978. I felt too depleted to be able to study and teach effectively. However, I missed it so much that I decided to resume teaching the following September. We were to study Romans, one of the more difficult books of the Bible.

I still missed Gene terribly, for he had been not only my husband and best friend, but also my spiritual mentor. I had always gone to him with any problem in my studying, and he explained things simply and beautifully. Even though I had kept all of his books, commentaries, and sermons for reference, I just didn't have him. I was unable to think clearly or to concentrate, and my teaching was cold and flat.

One dismal morning I sat at my desk and cried and cried. I felt like giving up. I told God I just didn't have what it took to teach. I told him that I believed in him, that I didn't feel rebellious about Gene's being called home, that I wanted to serve him and, above all, to be a witness to joy in the midst of hurt. But, I also told him, I couldn't bring myself to teach anymore.

As I often did when I was upset, I turned to the Bible and to the lesson I was working on. In the fourth chapter of Romans, verse 18, Paul writes, "Abraham in hope believed." In verses 13-16, Abraham received the promise and "the promise comes by faith." That gift, I knew, was available to me. I could experience God for myself and not just through Gene. I then developed a certainty and warmth, a joy and a confidence that I had not felt in months. I made a vow to ask God to help me with my teaching according to his promises. I committed my trust to him so that I could continue teaching. God renewed my trust in him and gave me an assurance of his abiding presence. I felt challenged to pick myself up and move forward.

Teaching has since been a blessing in so many ways—in the development of my faith, in my assurance that God is real, and in the sure knowledge that he loves me wherever I might be. I am confident that he will always be with me and sustain me. All I have to do is step out in faith, believe his promises, and trust him.

The Blessing of Marriage

The Lord God said, "It is not good for the man to be alone. I will make a helper suitable for him." So the Lord God caused the man to fall into a deep sleep; and while he was sleeping, he took one of the man's ribs and closed up the place with flesh. Then the Lord God made a woman from the rib he had taken out of the man, and he brought her to the man. The man said, "This is now bone of my bones and flesh of my flesh; she shall be called 'woman,' for she was taken out of man." For this reason a man will leave his father and mother and be united to his wife, and they will become one flesh.

Genesis 2:18, 21-24

"I'll Never Marry
A Preacher"

*In his heart a man plans his course,
but the Lord determines his steps.*
Proverbs 16:9

In 1930, I began to notice Gene when he came for a week of meetings in Greensboro, Georgia and wound up being a song-leader in my father's church. Since music was vital to me, I was touched by his natural and wonderful voice; it wasn't a trained voice but certainly one that could lead others in singing.

During the next year, I dated a friend of Gene's, a young seminarian named Ansley. Our relationship wasn't serious, but he was attractive and we had quite a nice time together. One day Gene called and said, "I'm coming to Greensboro for an appointment, and Ansley asked me to come by and have a talk with you." I was surprised, needless to say, and asked, "What about?" I was even more surprised when his reply was, "This thing you have about not marrying a preacher!" All I could muster up was, "Okay, I'll be ready for you."

Well, he stopped by, and I guess we had a date of sorts. We sat and talked on the porch for hours about being a preacher and being a preacher's wife.

We talked about the difficulties of being a minister's child and how we so frequently as children felt in the spotlight being called to live according to Christian beliefs, even though it appeared our friends could do anything they wanted.

I confided in him how happy I was in my family, though I constantly felt I was being watched and checked on for everything I did. I also told him that even though my mother was a great lady, strong in her beliefs and actions and a central part of our community, she was often misunderstood and criticized.

I ended the evening by stating, "You can tell Ansley

what you want, but I'm still never going to marry a preacher!"

Gene never told me what he said to Ansley, if anything, but he began to call me for dates, and our relationship gradually became easy and natural. I began to realize that God had overridden my own determined plans for the future and that I was going to have to eat my words, strong as they had been.

I knew, as I began to fall in love with Gene, that I was going to marry a preacher, and I would never be happy without him no matter what his calling might be.

Marrying Gene was the best decision I have ever made and was a true testimony to God's divine plan for the two of us. It was a strong lesson to me that no matter how confident and deliberate we might be in making our own plans for the future, God will change them in a heartbeat if they are not according to his design.

A Great Loss

Brothers we do not want you to be ignorant about those who fall asleep, or to grieve like the rest of men, who have no hope. We believe that Jesus died and rose again and so we believe that God will bring with Jesus those who have fallen asleep in him.

1 Thessalonians 4:13-14

Gene and I had been married for forty-eight years when he gradually became ill. At first he experienced a marked loss of energy that eventually led to a chronic cough, severe shortness of breath, and a growing conviction that the end was near. Yet he continued to persevere with great courage and dignity.

One afternoon Gene wanted to walk out to our backyard garden, which had been an important part of our lives for many decades. He was so physically weak that he was unable to rise from his chair. Alarmed, we knew something was terribly wrong and arranged for him to see his doctor immediately. Gene was hospitalized and tests revealed that he had advanced lung cancer. A heavy smoker nearly all his life, he had never been able to stop smoking for long no matter how hard he tried. Following agonizing periods of abstinence, I will never forget how he would weep each time he began smoking again. He honestly desired to give up such a life-altering habit, yet he just never could.

Although we were prepared for the probable diagnosis of lung cancer considering Gene's symptoms, this was a terribly sad time for our family.

I will never forget when he said to me, "I don't mind dying, 'Heart,' but I do hate to leave you." I think because it was such an emotional period in my life, I made a mistake that I came to regret. I sensed that he wanted to talk about the physical aspects of death, the process of dying and leaving those he loved, and the promise of life everlasting. It was so painful for me that I could not bring myself to participate in those conversations. I desperately tried to be brave in order to help him be brave, yet I would give anything if I could take back all of my worries over the concerns of the moment and instead have spoken the thoughts that would have most helped us both in his last days and hours. It is a comfort that we were able to read the Bible and to pray together. In one of those prayer times together, Gene asked God to accept his life and the things he had tried to do as a minister of Jesus Christ. He quietly died two weeks later.

One great comfort to me was that I had Gene far longer than I ever thought I would. When he retired in 1966, his health was not particularly good, and I prayed over and over, "God, let him live at least one year before you take him." God let him live a full twelve years, and we had such marvelous times together. It was the only period in our marriage that we were able to be together with only the normal demands of daily life.

During the difficult grieving period following Gene's death, I felt determined to be a witness to God's faithful presence in my life. I felt incredibly blessed with great strength to handle such a personal and deeply painful loss and I certainly didn't take this gift of faith for granted.

During the times of the day when I was away from home, I tried always to be strong and not break down in front of others. However, I came to realize that when I was at home by myself, it was all right to let the tears and anger come where no one could hear me. Many nights when I couldn't sleep, it helped to play the piano—sometimes for hours and hours.

I attempted to begin teaching piano and weekly Sunday school classes again, neither of which went very well in the beginning. The very mention of Gene's name caused me to break down in an uncontrollable flood of tears.

My friends were helpful and supportive, and I willingly followed every suggestion made to me during those first few months, especially those made by my widowed friends. One friend suggested that I get out with other people as much as possible each day and save my housework for the interminable evenings in order to have something to occupy my time. It was an exhausting but effective schedule!

Spending time in my beautiful garden and reading scripture comforted me greatly. The Bible gave me hope that I otherwise would not have had. Over and over, I kept remembering Paul's words from Romans 8:38:

> For I am convinced that neither death nor life, neither angels nor demons, neither the present nor the future, nor any powers, neither height nor depth, nor anything else in all creation, will be able to separate us from the love of God that is in Christ Jesus our Lord.

Gradually, the healing began, and I seemed to grow up spiritually and emotionally. I began to teach better and to study better. And my prayer life deepened because I turned to God rather than to Gene or another person to help me straighten out a problem or understand something in one of my Sunday school lessons. But how I missed Gene! He had been a wonderful leader, strong and patient, and if I needed any advice with my lessons, the church, our children, or our neighborhood concerns, he always talked to me with wisdom and a sense of humor. He was almost always right in his counsel, and I missed him terribly.

Learning to live without him had seemed impossible, yet God graciously surrounded me and uplifted me through my children, grandchildren and my church. God's faithful presence following the loss of my beloved husband, convinced me that absolutely nothing can ever separate us from God's love in Jesus Christ. On this truth I build my life.

A YARDMAN AND A COOK

Every good and perfect gift is from above.
JAMES 1:17

It had been six years since Gene's death, and I was finally happy again, having gradually adjusted to being alone. One afternoon Fred Jones, an old friend of ours from church, called to ask if he might come by to discuss a problem. "Sure," I said. "I can make us a ham sandwich and a glass of iced tea, and I'd love for you to join me for lunch." I didn't think anything was unusual about his call since he and his wife, Violet, now deceased, had been members of my Sunday school class for many years. While I certainly wasn't a counselor, I could listen sympathetically and hold a confidence.

Not long after we had talked, Fred came by with

some fresh fruit to thank me for having him for lunch. Subsequently, we began to talk with one another more often, and gradually the friendship grew a little more personal. He would often come to rake the leaves in my front yard. Having lived in an apartment for some time, he longed to be active outdoors. After walking a mile or two each morning, he would stop by to work in my yard for a while, even when I wasn't home. How wonderful it was to pull into my driveway and find big piles of freshly raked leaves. My yard was full of oaks, maples, and hickory trees that shed generously every fall, and as much as I loved to rake them up, I was always behind.

One day I came home not only to raked leaves, but to a loaf of bread and a package of spaghetti at my front door. I suspected it was Fred, and I called him as soon as I walked in the door to ask if he was the "culprit." "Yes," he said. "There was a two-for-one sale when I went to the grocery store today, so I decided to bring you the free one."

Not long after, I laughingly told my daughter, Beth, a few "Fred stories" as we were chatting on the phone one evening. You can't imagine my surprise when, instead of laughing in return, she said, "Mother, Fred is courting you." "No!" I proclaimed a little defensively. "No one would ever think about courting a seventy-eight-year-old woman." The thought had never entered my mind. However, when he asked me out for Sunday dinner a few days later, I found myself thinking, maybe Beth was right.

As we began to see each other more frequently, I decided it would be in our best interest not to be seen together at church, so we went to the services and meetings separately. We wouldn't even drive home together. I would drive myself home and then he would come over afterward. As we began to dine out more often, we kept seeking restaurants that were not in our area so that we wouldn't run into anyone that we knew. It actually was kind of an exciting time for two rather mature people!

It seemed as if our relationship was growing steadily more serious, but this progression was very, very gradual. That is, until one night when we were sitting in my den talking, and suddenly Fred stopped mid-sentence, looked at me, and said, "Martha, I love you." I didn't mean to, but I looked at him as if he was slightly crazy. While I don't remember exactly what my response was, I clearly remember changing the subject, leaving his words hanging.

The following spring, I drove to Kentucky for a few days with two of my old Agnes Scott friends. When we arrived back in Atlanta, a terrible storm had ripped through the city, uprooting trees and causing widespread power outages. Huge limbs had downed telephone and power lines, and it was a real challenge to get back into my house. Fred called immediately to make sure I was all right.

We were both without power, and neither of us had any food that didn't require cooking, so he offered to drive through the debris-laden streets to pick me up for dinner at the Piccadilly Cafeteria. Roads were closed and everywhere there were downed trees. Before we got to Peachtree Road, less than a mile away, he had proposed to me! I will never forget turning to him and asking if he really thought marriage at our ages might work, or if it could even last. I was seventy-eight years old, and Fred was eighty-four.

Following a long silence, I managed to say, "We can talk about this if you want to, but right now, I don't know what my answer will be."

We were able to talk openly about nearly everything. The fact that we could talk about important matters quietly and honestly had a great deal to do with me finally being able to say, "I will be happy to be your wife." Fred was a lovely Christian gentleman who was open and honest. I felt incredibly blessed to have another chance to have a loving relationship at my age.

For several weeks we talked over many concerns such as sex, finances, our families, children, and our grandchildren until we finally felt comfortable with our decision to marry.

Marriage at this stage of our lives represented enormous adjustments. We both were enjoying a certain independence and freedom for the first time in many decades. Music was an integral part of my life and Fred was not musically inclined. I was committed to teaching the Bible, which had been the most important part of my life since childhood, and Fred had only a marginal interest in biblical and spiritual matters. However, we belonged to the same church, had many of the same friends, loved to garden, and both of us wanted to live in my house. Fred was very clear about what each of us should be able to do financially.

There is a huge difference in marrying when you are in your twenties and marrying when you are seventy-eight and eighty-four. You look at life so differently when you are older. We didn't have to think about having children, building a home, or worrying about the future because the future was already with us. We did have to consider the fact that we were both older, retired, and would be in each other's company for most of every day.

After all our soul searching, we couldn't have been more excited over our upcoming marriage. I still laugh about the day we got our marriage license. We went downtown to City Hall, a huge place filled with mostly younger people. We had to stand in line to take a number before being called to fill out the necessary documents. After our number was called, Fred and I approached the window, keenly aware that the employees had begun to giggle quietly. As we rotated from one window to the next in order to complete the registration for our marriage license, they broke into hilarious laughter. Puzzled, Fred asked, "What in the world are you laughing about?" The unanimous answer was, "Y'all are too old to be getting married!"

Our engagement was officially announced not long after at a Sunday school picnic. It was so completely unexpected, as I had not yet received my engagement ring. Fred and I felt the announcement was a bit premature. We were somewhat anxious about how our news would be accepted by our friends and acquaintances, yet our closest friends were convinced that the time was perfect. As it turned out, they were right.

Shortly after the announcement, someone came up to me in the church hall and said, "Martha, I didn't know you wanted to remarry." I spontaneously replied, "Well, neither did I, but I needed a yardman." When I told this to Fred, his comment was, "That's okay, because I needed a cook!"

Fred died shortly before his hundredth birthday. Before we married, we had discussed the fact that because of our ages, we might have only a brief time together. We had decided though, that if we had five to seven years together, it would be worth the adjustment. God, in his goodness, gave us fifteen years full of incredible blessings and endless joy.

The Blessing of Prayer

*Then you will call upon me and come and pray to me, and
I will listen to you. You will seek me and find me when
you seek me with all your heart.*
                              Jeremiah 29:12-13

THE MIRACLE
OF ANSWERED PRAYERS

*This is the confidence we have in approaching God: that if
we ask anything according to his will, he hears us. And if
we know that he hears us—whatever we ask—we know
that we have what we asked of him.*
I JOHN 5:14-15

In 1953, our family witnessed a true miracle of healing that left us without adequate words of gratitude to God. Our son, Gene Jr., had been stricken with polio at the age of sixteen. This was a heartbreaking and uncertain time in our lives, yet we were all miraculously comforted and sustained by a love that was beyond anything we had ever experienced.

Gene Jr. was a counselor at a YMCA summer camp when he became ill. Looking back, I realize it was by God's grace that our entire family was staying at the camp during that week. Gene Sr. had been asked to be the minister in residence, and we had been invited to accompany him as a part of his compensation for serving as camp minister.

When we suspected young Gene might have polio, we took him from the camp infirmary to a small local hospital where the frightening diagnosis was made. Immediately we drove him back to Atlanta. Beth and Peggy, our daughters, huddled in the front seat with their father, while Gene, Jr. was stretched out on the back seat with me, his head cradled in my lap. He was in great pain and appeared to be very weak. I was terrified of what lay ahead of us and the haunting possibilities kept racing through my head. I could do nothing but pray and try to comfort my son in any small way I possibly could. Where in the world, I wondered, was our Heavenly Father?

At that time, the old Grady hospital in Atlanta was the only facility with an available room capable of caring for a polio victim. Gene was admitted as soon as we arrived there, and that was to be the last physical contact we had with him for ten days. He had to be placed in isolation.

I couldn't bear being unable to see my son during such a critical time of his illness. With a mother's determination I devised a plan just to see him even if I couldn't physically be in the room with him. I snooped around the outside of the building and discovered a small window at the top of his ground floor room. I knew Gene wasn't able to sit up and look out the window so I figured out a way that I could look in! Each morning he was at Grady, I visited him by packing an old kitchen stool in the back of my car, driving to the hospital, and finding the closest possible parking space to his room.

I then dragged the stool to his open window, climbed up on it and talked to him, telling him how much I loved him.

I will never forget my first "visit" with Gene. I stood on the rickety stool, my heart in my throat, and talked to him with every bit of love in my being. He tried so hard to turn his head in response to my voice, but he simply did not have the strength. Seeing a bowl of untouched grits on the table by his bed infuriated me because Gene was unable to feed himself. It was obvious no staff member was available to feed him. Never had I felt so helpless. It seemed as if my heart would break. The despair and grief seemed almost too much to bear.

One Sunday morning, a few days later, I left the hospital in time to get to church for the eleven o'clock service and once there, I fell apart. All that had happened was too devastating. I tried so hard to sing the familiar hymns and to absorb the words of Gene Sr.'s sermon, yet I was too overwhelmed. The warm embraces from dear friends who loved us loosened all of my emotions, and I could not stop crying.

Questions began to fly through my mind. Why, I wondered, had this happened to our only son? Gene was so special. We had wanted our third child to be a boy, and we were beyond grateful at his birth. I kept asking God if we had thought young Gene was too special. Had we loved him unwisely? Had we loved him too much, forgetting to praise God with thanksgiving? I couldn't control my thoughts and questions. My heart was absolutely pierced and there is still a feeling of anguish when I reflect on that time in our lives.

Yet God began to work in the most amazing ways. Once word got out that Gene had polio and was at Grady Hospital, our congregation rallied behind us. They immediately called an impromptu prayer session, praying for Gene's healing and for our family. I believe, from the bottom of my heart, that my strength to persevere during this time of sorrow came because God was at work through these wonderful people. Knowing that our friends were lifting us up in prayer gave me a great deal of emotional security at a time when I was both fragile and very frightened.

I was also beginning to learn how God uses and works though his people to help others. While I prayed with agonizing fervor, I felt as if my prayers were not getting any higher than the ceiling.

Yet Christ was present in his people. Although God did not appear to me in any kind of miraculous way, or suddenly emerge from a swirl of clouds, or speak with extraordinary voices, I felt his steady presence. The constant prayers of others gave me strength, courage, and an ability to face each day with hope.

Following his discharge from Grady, Gene had a brief stay at Emory University Hospital. After a thorough physical evaluation, the doctors told us they had reserved a room for him at the Warm Springs Foundation in Georgia, a facility established by Franklin D. Roosevelt, following his paralyzing bout with polio in the 1940s. It had been discovered that polio victims benefited dramatically when regularly submerged in the warm mineral springs. A number of other services were provided by the doctors and therapists who specialized in treating patients with paralytic conditions.

Gene's doctors were certain he needed to be in such a therapeutic environment. They had prepared us for that eventuality, explaining that he most likely would have to be in an iron lung (a chamber-like respirator). I will never forget anxiously awaiting the call from his doctors at Emory, certain he would have to be moved to Warm Springs.

When the miracle call came telling us it wouldn't be necessary for him to be transferred to Warm Springs, and that he would be able to come home soon, Gene Sr., the girls, and I put our arms around each other right there in our little hallway. We danced, sang, and rejoiced, and as we embraced, Gene prayed a heartfelt prayer of thanksgiving.

The miracle of answered prayers continued as young Gene began to heal. God provided abundantly during Gene's slow and difficult recuperation. We never lacked for people to drive him back and forth to Emory University Hospital for the vigorous rehabilitation he had to undergo. Their help enabled me to take care of his daily exercises and therapy at home.

Gene Sr. was soon at work again, bringing home laughter and love to all of us. With his support and encouragement I was finally becoming able to accept our son's debilitating illness.

My prayer that God would bring goodness and hope through all of the sadness and trauma we had experienced had been answered in many ways. We had been surrounded by the love of friends; Gene did not have to go to Warm Springs; he did not have to be in an iron lung; he was not permanently paralyzed, and eventually he was able to live a normal life.

When he became ill, all these things had seemed impossible. Yet God unfailingly revealed himself through the love and warmth of his people by answering the many prayers that had been lifted up on behalf of young Gene and our family.

His healing was truly a miracle—a loving answer from God to the cries of his faithful people.

The Blessing of Suffering

*I consider that our present sufferings are not worth
comparing with the glory that will be revealed in us.*

Romans 8:18

My First Real Sorrow

[God] comforts us in all our troubles, so that we can comfort those in any trouble with the comfort we ourselves have received from God.

2 Corinthians 1:4

In the fall of 1950, I was thoroughly enjoying life as a wife, mother, and teacher. I was in my mid-forties and felt that God had blessed me abundantly. Secure in my faith and in the love of my husband and children, I felt confident that all was well with life. That was until I received a devastating phone call from my brother Frank, a physician in Winston-Salem, North Carolina.

It was a lovely fall day, warm and breezy, and I had thrown open every window in our little manse to the warmth and fresh air of the day. I had just come in from raking up the golden leaves of the hickory tree in our front yard and was fixing a glass of iced tea when the phone rang. I will never forget how startled I was to hear a man's sobbing voice at the other end of the line. Then Frank began to speak, haltingly, tearfully explaining that our beloved sister Elizabeth, "Libby," had been stricken with a strain of leukemia that would prove fatal.

Stunned, I sank into the chair next to our little telephone table, barely able to catch my breath, as my brother continued to talk and sob. I was numb, yet my mind raced as I tried to absorb such shocking news. The last I had heard from Libby was that she and her husband of two years were trying to conceive their first baby. I had gloried in this news from my twenty-nine-year-old sister, as I had gloried in every event of her life.

Libby was a talented musician, married to the chief music arranger for the Rockettes in New York City. It seemed as if their future was golden. Hadn't she always been the bright star in our lives? She was our baby, the youngest of the five of us. I was sixteen when she was born and had mothered her as if she were my own. We were truly kindred spirits. I couldn't take it all in; the sorrow was too great.

Thus began two very difficult years of my life as I lived daily with the awareness that Libby was suffering physically, emotionally, and spiritually— and I was powerless to change any aspect of her condition. Only God could heal, and the fact that he didn't heal her jolted every part of my being. My emotions ranged from anger to profound grief, and the fact that she was so far away only compounded my jumbled feelings.

We were rarely able to speak by phone because long distance charges were exorbitant for a minister's meager income, and frequent trips to New York were simply out of the question. I lay in bed at night sobbing and praying, sobbing because we were losing her and praying to understand why she was being taken before her life was ever fully lived. I already missed her dreadfully.

Finally, in early June a few months before her death, I was able to take the train to New York for what would be our final time together. The long train ride gave me an opportunity for prayer and quiet reflection. What should I say to her, or how could we discuss God and his prevailing mercy knowing that Libby's own faith had been ebbing for many years? It was cool and drizzling when I arrived in New York, and my mood was somber as I anxiously approached their tiny apartment.

When I entered her room, Libby appeared frail and very tired, yet her entire countenance lit up as I approached her bed. I could still detect a bright sparkle of love and intelligence in her face as our visit began. She had so many questions for which I had so few answers, and I feared that I was doing her soul more harm than good. Yet she reassured me time and again that my own faith was a boost and a comfort to her.

My visit ended far too soon, and I departed with my heart simply bursting with love for my dear sister. With her husband and our mother at her bedside, Libby passed away a few months later.

During the course of my grieving following Libby's death, God revealed a number of things to me that matured my faith in spite of my deep sorrow and confusion over such a great loss. It seemed impossible that I could both grieve and grow simultaneously, yet I did in ways beyond my own comprehension.

God, in his tender mercy, taught me the importance of reaching out to others as they grieve the loss of a loved one. He gave me a deep and abiding compassion for those who are hurting, which I would never have experienced had it not been for my own great loss.

THE DEEP PRUNING:
A MOTHER'S HEARTBREAK

"Father, if you are willing, take this cup from me; yet not my will but yours be done."

LUKE 22:42

I will never understand how any of us can work through our anger with God when a terrible injustice has occurred, yet I have come to trust that he is present even in the most devastating circumstances. Our middle child, Peggy, suffered a nearly fatal stroke when she was only fifty-three years old. She had endured many trials during her life and I felt as if she had bravely overcome them through perseverance and her deep faith. For her to be stricken in such a terrible way was almost more than I could bear.

Peggy had married a seminary student during the spring vacation of her senior year at Agnes Scott, and shortly thereafter, she and her husband, Tom, began their family. Their second son was born with cerebral palsy which brought great sorrow to Peggy. She and Tom had two more children, but the struggles of life eventually led to a divorce when their youngest was in high school.

Peggy was in her forties when she so unexpectedly found herself looking for a job. Music was a vital part of her life, so she took a position as a choir director in a small church. However, her salary barely provided for the needs of her family. She decided to attend seminary in order to improve her teaching skills, hoping this move would enhance her income opportunities.

Once she was established at Columbia Seminary in Decatur, Georgia, her professors began strongly encouraging her to become a minister, telling her that preaching was her gift. She taught so naturally and with such inspiration. She had a deep sense of the mystery of God and an uncanny ability to feel his presence in all situations.

During those years Peggy was balancing school with family life and it was an especially grueling time. She had three college-age children and a handicapped son at home, yet she managed to graduate with honors, tenth out of a class of 113, with top grades in Greek, Hebrew, and other studies. This was quite an accomplishment, and we were very proud of her.

Peggy became an ordained minister in 1985 at a time when churches were not quite ready for women in the clergy. Furthermore, she had three strikes against her. Not only was she a woman, but she was still caring for a handicapped son, and more notably she was the divorced wife of a minister. Two difficult and frustrating years passed before she was finally called to a small Presbyterian church in Greenville, South Carolina. The minister there was older and genuinely delighted to have Peggy on board.

Needless to say, she was thrilled to finally have a church and to be given the opportunity to work with fewer constraints. She was there for eighteen months before her stroke and, I must say, I had never seen her happier.

I learned of Peggy's stroke when her son Tommy, who was in graduate school at Yale, called me at two o'clock in the morning. I was eighty-one years old, and Fred, whom I had recently married, was eighty-seven, so driving at that hour was out of the question. Some of the longest hours I have ever lived through were those between Tommy's call at two a.m. and our frantic departure at dawn's first light.

As I agonized over my child's precarious situation that long night, I was simply unable to comprehend (until much later) that God was as present with Peggy during the hours she lay alone and unconscious as he was on the cross with Christ. Since that time, I've come to believe that God was more bereft than I, for he loved Peggy far more than I could ever love her.

The very minute we felt it was safe enough to drive, Fred and I left for Greenville. I insisted on driving because I felt such a desperate need to be in control in some small way, and I must say that I drove in record time. Thankfully, there was very little traffic in those early hours.

As we approached Greenville, I realized that we had no idea what hospital Peggy was in; I felt helpless, overwhelmed, and exhausted. Even in the midst of terrible trials, I've come to understand that God has a way of mapping our course when we least expect it. As we approached the city, we saw a blue and white sign with arrows pointing the direction to a hospital. We anxiously followed the marker, praying that we were heading in the right direction.

I was somehow able to park the car and the two of us rushed into the front entrance to the desk in the lobby, not only afraid that we were at the wrong hospital but deeply concerned that we were running out of time because of Peggy's critical condition. As we identified ourselves, the front desk attendant said they had been expecting us and arranged for us to be taken to the recovery room right away.

The entire hospital staff could not have been kinder to us, which was a blessing because it helped to ease our fear and our anxiety about Peggy's desperate situation. Fred and I sat next to Peggy's bed for quite awhile that morning, wanting so badly for her to know that we were present. I will always believe that, through God, Peggy was aware of my love for her during those critical hours following her surgery.

After some time, Fred and I left Peggy's bedside to sit in the intensive care waiting room. When we stepped off the elevator, two women from her church were standing there and immediately recognized us, even though we had never met them. They introduced themselves, ushered us into the ICU waiting room, and gave us a thorough briefing on everything that had happened. Those dear ladies had been at the hospital for hours and were the primary contacts for her doctors until family members could get there. What a beautiful blessing they were to all of us.

Blessings seemed to pour over us in so many ways. As Peggy's children began to arrive, members of her congregation poured into the little hospital waiting area, loving and caring for us in every conceivable way. While it was such a frightening time for Peggy and our family, it was also a beautiful time. So many people were praying for us and God's love continuously washed over us in the most unexpected ways.

For more than a decade following the stroke, Peggy experienced grand mal seizures, a condition directly related to the stroke and one that could not be medically controlled. She suffered blinding headaches, along with other stroke-related disabilities, and became increasingly incapacitated, discouraged, and exhausted.

It was at this point that divine intervention occurred. Peggy's sister, Beth, learned of a group of doctors who specialized in working with stroke victims who had been incapacitated for a number of years.

Until then, none of us held much hope for Peggy's rehabilitation. The original team of doctors who saved her life had informed our family that stroke victims who were not treated immediately usually incurred permanent paralysis. Peggy had been without medical assistance for many hours following her stroke.

The commitment to intensive therapy had begun again, but this time with more hope. Miracles have continued to happen with Peggy's unexpected improvement. She is able to get out more and is going to church once again. Her speech and motor skills continue to improve and she has even become a mentor to a friend who, because of a stroke, is incapable of communicating.

All of the things Peggy excelled in were lost to her after the stroke and, even today, she speaks very haltingly and slowly. She can neither read nor write, and of course, she cannot preach. Not long ago, I asked Peggy if she felt any bitterness. She replied, "Oh, Mother, I did, but I'm over it now."

I too have finally accepted Peggy's illness. The anger that I had experienced for so long, the arguing with God,

and the "why my Peggy?" questions have gradually sub-
sided. God has helped me to grow to a place of accep-
tance, and I am finally able to say to God sincerely, "Thy
will be done."

Epilogue

A FULL HARVEST

"This is what the Kingdom of God is like. A man scatters seed on the ground. Night and day, whether he sleeps or gets up, the seed sprouts and grows, though he does not know how. All by itself the soil produces grain, first the stalk, then the head, then the full kernel in the head. As soon as the grain is ripe, he puts the sickle to it, because the harvest has come."

MARK 4: 26-29

Our time of listening to stories from our beloved friend had come to an end. We asked Martha, "If you knew the Lord was calling you home tomorrow and you could leave only one message for family and friends, what would it be?" She had lived almost a full century, and we eagerly anticipated her answer.

Her response to us was simple and timeless. "Make room for Jesus Christ in your life. By doing so, you've hitched your wagon to a star and not to a triviality."

She went on to say that life must have a center. "When you have Christ as your center and you earnestly desire to honor him, everything else will follow. By abiding in him, we have the indwelling of the Holy Spirit. We become beneficiaries of his strength and courage so necessary for us each day. With God's standards as the guide, our gifts are revealed, our love for others becomes different, and our goals take on an eternal perspective. Our purpose in living transcends the trivialities that so often take on an inflated and unimportant perspective which reflects the cultural standards of today."

Martha's message was so simple, yet so profound. Its simplicity applies to all ages and to all walks of life, and its power is timeless.

The blessings of Martha's own backyard extend far beyond her garden walls. Through her lifelong commitment to teaching, she has planted countless seeds. Through her unfailing love for others, she has nourished the growth of Christian discipleship. Through her strength of character and extraordinary personal example, she has lovingly shaped the lives of innumerable individuals.

God alone knows the full impact of Martha's faithful planting, nourishing, and tending. However, it seems obvious to those who know and love her that her harvest will be full, rich, and plentiful. In God's good time she will certainly hear the Master's voice saying, "Well done, good and faithful servant!" (Matthew 25:23)

Marianne Craft
Hyland Justice
Ree Hoffman
Nancy McGuirk
RuthAnn Skinner

Martha's Prayer

Dear Father,

I thank you for your grace that has claimed me, your patience that walks with me, your forgiveness that cleanses and restores me, but most of all for your love that holds me close and will never let me go. Please accept my adoration and praise.

In the name of Jesus,

Amen

For additional copies of this book, please contact:
Peachtree Presbyterian Book Store
Peachtree Presbyterian Church
3434 Roswell Road, N.W.
Atlanta, Georgia   30305
404-842-3169